Seven Wonders of
SPACE
PHENOMENA

D. J. Ward

TWENTY-FIRST CENTURY BOOKS
Minneapolis

To J, S, D, C, B, W, E, M, and L:
nine wonders of the universe

Photo Acknowledgments

The images in this book are used with the permission of: © Chad Baker/The Image Banky/Getty Images, p. 5; ESA/NASA/SOHO, pp. 6, 13 (bottom), 14; © Chesterf/Dreamstime.com, p. 7; © Laura Westlund/Independent Picture Service, pp. 8, 13 (top); International Astronomical Union, p. 9; © Feng Yu/Dreamstime.com, p. 10 (top); © Haveseen/Dreamstime.com, p. 10 (bottom); NASA/JPL-Caltech, pp. 11, 18, 24, 57, 73 (bottom left); © Jeffrey Coolidge/Digital Vision/Getty Images, p. 12; © Pascal/Dreamstime.com, pp. 13 (background), 38; © Ron Miller, pp. 16, 17, 22, 43, 52, 59, 62; NASA/CXC/A. Zezas et al., p. 19; © Jennifer Russell/Dreamstime.com, p. 20; © iStockphoto.com/Pete Collins, p. 21; © Jean-Pierre Clatot/AFP/Getty Images, p. 25; NASA/CXC/M. Weiss, p. 26; © Mehau Kulyk/Photo Researchers, Inc., p. 28; © Ilya Postnikov/Dreamstime.com, pp. 29, 73 (bottom right); © Imagno/Hulton Archive/Getty Images, p. 30 (top); © Stock Montage/Archive Photos/Getty Images, p. 30 (bottom); NASA/JPL, Caltech/WISE, p. 31; NASA/JPL, pp. 32, 54, 69, 73 (bottom center); © Margaret Bourke-White/Time & Life Pictures/Getty Images, p. 34; © David Levenson/Getty Images, p. 35; © Thinkstock/Comstock Images/Getty Images, p. 36; NASA/WMAP Science Team, p. 37; © Chris Harvey/Stone/Getty Images, p. 39; NASA, ESA, and The Hubble Heritage Team (STScI/AURA)/Hubble Collaboration, p. 40; © Bettmann/CORBIS, p. 41; © Brookhaven National Laboratory / Photo Researchers, Inc., p. 44 (left); © SPL/Photo Researchers, Inc., p. 44 (right); X-ray: NASA/CXC/M.Markevitch et al. Optical: NASA/STScI; Magellan/U.Arizona/D .Clowe et al. Lensing Map: NASA/STScI; ESO WFI; Magellan/U.Arizona/D .Clowe et al., p. 46; © Image Source/Getty Images, p. 47; ESO, p. 48; © Mark Garlick/Photo Researchers, Inc., p. 51; Paramount/The Kobal Collection, p. 55; NASA/CXC/SAO, p. 56; © Alfred Eisenstaedt/Time & Life Pictures/Getty Images, p. 60; NASA, pp. 63, 68; © Tetra Images/Getty Images, p. 65 (top); NASA/JPL-Caltech/ASU, pp. 65 (bottom), 73 (top left); © Photolibrary/Getty Images, p. 66 (inset); © Matthew Oldfield/Alamy, p. 66 (main); NASA/GSFC, p. 67; ESA/V. Beckmann (NASA-GSFC), p. 73 (top center); © Jean-Francois Podevin/Photo Researchers, Inc., p. 73 (top right); NASA/MSFC, p. 73 (center right).

Front cover: ESA/V. Beckmann (NASA-GSFC) (top left); NASA/JPL-Caltech (top center); © Jean-Francois Podevin/Photo Researchers, Inc. (top right); NASA/JPL NASA/MSFC (center); © Ilya Postnikov/Dreamstime.com (bottom left); NASA/JPL-Caltech/ASU (bottom center); NASA/JPL (bottom right).

Twenty-First Century Books
A division of Lerner Publishing Group, Inc.
241 First Avenue North
Minneapolis, MN 55401 U.S.A.

Website address: www.lernerbooks.com

Ward, David J.
        Seven wonders of space phenomena / by D.J. Ward.
             p.   cm. — (Seven wonders)
        Includes bibliographical references and index.
        ISBN 978–0–7613–5452–9 (lib. bdg. : alk. paper)
        1. Astronomy—Miscellanea—Juvenile literature. I. Title.
    QB46.W246 2011
    520—dc22   2010028447

Manufactured in the United States of America
1 – DP – 12/31/10

Contents

INTRODUCTION

$\mathcal{P}$EOPLE LOVE TO MAKE LISTS OF THE BIGGEST AND THE BEST. ALMOST TWENTY-FIVE HUNDRED YEARS AGO, A GREEK WRITER NAMED HERODOTUS MADE A LIST OF THE MOST AWESOME THINGS EVER BUILT BY PEOPLE. THE LIST INCLUDED BUILDINGS, STATUES, AND OTHER OBJECTS THAT WERE LARGE, WONDROUS, AND IMPRESSIVE. LATER, OTHER WRITERS ADDED NEW ITEMS TO THE LIST. WRITERS EVENTUALLY AGREED ON A FINAL LIST. IT WAS CALLED THE SEVEN WONDERS OF THE ANCIENT WORLD.

The list became so famous that people began imitating it. They made other lists of wonders. They listed the Seven Wonders of the Modern World and the Seven Wonders of the Middle Ages. People also made lists of wonders of science and technology.

A PHENOMENAL UNIVERSE

But if you're looking to be truly in awe, there's no better place to look than space. The shining Sun and twinkling stars make space seem pleasant and familiar. But, in fact, space is home to breathtaking power and mind-blowing mystery. Our universe is nothing short of phenomenal, or extraordinary.

The more we discover about space, the more we realize how little we understand. New discoveries raise more questions than they answer. Even astronomers, scientists who study space, don't know about most of the universe. They don't even understand much about the Sun, the star in our own neighborhood.

This photograph, taken from space, shows Earth with the Sun in the background. The solar system and the universe beyond are full of wonders as well as mysteries.

OUT OF THIS WORLD

This book is about Seven Wonders of Space Phenomena—or phenomenal things in space. The following chapters will try to answer some tough questions: What would happen if you fell into a black hole? What was our universe like in the beginning? How will the universe end? Will humans ever be able to travel across the universe? Could we ever travel through time? Is Earth the only planet with life, or is the universe teeming with life-forms?

We live in a universe rich with mystery. The mystery is what makes space so hard to resist. In the following pages, prepare to leave behind what is familiar. Prepare to feel small. Prepare to be amazed.

THE EXTRAORDINARY
Sun

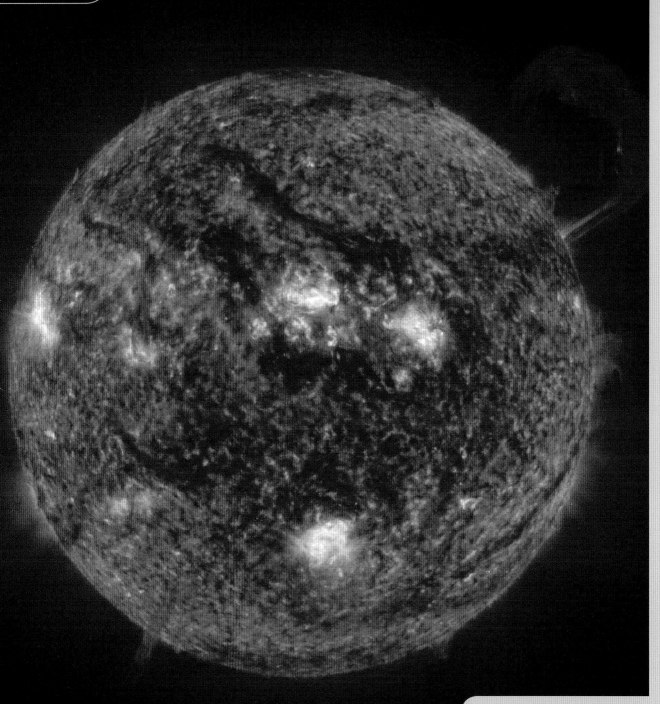

This image shows the Sun close-up. The picture shows streams of gases shooting out into space.

STAND OUTSIDE AND HOLD A DIME OUT AT ARM'S LENGTH. WITH THAT DIME, YOU COULD COVER UP THE SUN. IT TAKES UP ONLY A SMALL PORTION OF OUR SKY. BUT THE SUN IS BIG—REALLY BIG. SET SIDE BY SIDE, IT WOULD TAKE 109 EARTHS TO STRETCH ACROSS THE ENTIRE WIDTH OF THE SUN.

The Sun isn't just big—it's a big deal. The Sun is the energy source for life on our planet. It provides the energy that makes plants grow. It provides just the right amount of warmth to keep our oceans from freezing solid or drying up. Without the Sun, you wouldn't be here.

Our planet depends on the Sun's energy. Its warmth and light make life possible on Earth.

> *"The Sun is the only astronomical object that critically matters to humankind."*
>
> —*U. S. astronomer John Harvey, 2004*

MAKING SUNSHINE

The Sun is composed mostly of hydrogen. Like all matter, or stuff, hydrogen is made up of tiny particles called atoms. Atoms contain even smaller particles called protons, neutrons, and electrons. Hydrogen atoms are the simplest atoms in the universe. Most atoms contain several protons, neutrons, and electrons. But a hydrogen atom contains only one proton and one electron.

The atoms at the surface of the Sun are very loosely packed. The deeper you go into the Sun, the tighter the atoms are compressed. A force called gravity squeezes the atoms tightly together. The more tightly matter is compressed, the denser and heavier it becomes. Squeezing matter tightly also raises its temperature. The temperature at the Sun's core, or center, is 27,000,000°F (15,000,000°C).

In the Sun's core, gravity squeezes hydrogen atoms so tightly that they fuse together. The atoms don't just connect to one another. Their parts combine to make an entirely different substance: helium. Helium atoms are bigger than hydrogen atoms.

Combining atoms to build a larger kind of atom is called nuclear fusion. Nuclear fusion destroys a little bit of matter and turns it into pure energy.

Atoms are the building blocks of matter. The nucleus, or center, of an atom holds neutrons and protons. Electrons travel around the nucleus. Different kinds of atoms have different numbers of neutrons, protons, and electrons.

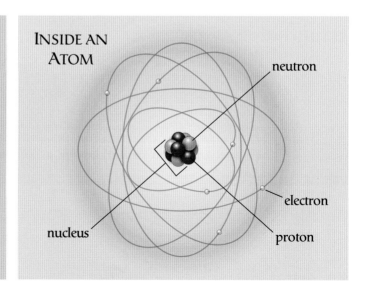

INSIDE AN ATOM

neutron

electron

nucleus

proton

MERCURY VENUS EARTH MARS JUPITER SATURN URANUS NEPTUNE

SUN

CERES PLUTO ERIS

PLANETS

DWARF PLANETS

The solar system consists of our Sun and everything that travels around it, including the planets and their moons. The Sun contains 99.8 percent of all the matter in our solar system.

It's a *Fact*

In 1905 German physicist Albert Einstein's wrote a famous equation: $E = mc^2$. The equation says that energy (E) equals a body's mass (m; the amount of matter a body contains) multiplied by the speed of light (c) squared, or multiplied by itself. The equation describes how much energy is released when matter is converted into energy, such as during nuclear fusion.

Inside the Sun, the little bit of matter that is destroyed turns into a bundle of light called a photon.

Light produced in the Sun's core begins to travel outward. However, the Sun's interior is so dense that it's hard for photons to escape. Each photon bounces randomly from atom to atom until it finds its way out of the Sun. Each one follows a different path. Each one takes a different amount of time to make it from the core to the Sun's surface. Some photons may take more than one million years to reach the surface. Sunlight that shines on you each day is old. It traveled for years before it even left the Sun.

The Extraordinary Sun

A Burning Ball of *Plasma*

The Sun is just a burning ball of gas in space, right? Actually, the Sun is not gas. It's made of plasma, a kind of matter. Matter can take one of several forms. It can be solid, such as rock. It can be a liquid, such as water. It can be a gas, such as the air we breathe. But most of the matter in the universe is not solid, liquid, or gas. Almost all matter in the universe takes the form of plasma. Plasma is what you get when you heat up a gas.

When a gas gets hot enough, electrons circling around an atom's nucleus, or center, break free. The electrons begin floating around on their own, separate from any particular atom. Atoms that no longer have the right number of electrons are called ions. The matter that used to be gas becomes a mixed-up soup of ions and free-floating electrons. It becomes plasma.

If plasma is so common, why haven't most people heard of it? Actually, plasma isn't very common on Earth. We almost never encounter plasma in everyday life. But you can find plasma if you know where to look. Plasma is what makes fluorescent lightbulbs glow. Plasma puts the flash in lightning. Some flat-screen televisions use plasma to create pictures.

A few consumer products, such as fluorescent lightbulbs and flat-screen TVs, produce plasma. The Sun is made of plasma, a substance that results from the heating up of gas.

This image reveals the corona, the outermost layer of the Sun's atmosphere. The corona is hotter than the surface of the Sun.

THE CORONA

Imagine sitting at a campfire and finding that the air is much hotter 10 feet (3 meters) away from the flames than right next to them. That wouldn't make sense. But that's exactly what happens on the Sun.

The Sun is surrounded by a layer of gas and plasma. This layer is called the solar atmosphere. You would expect the solar atmosphere to get cooler the farther away you go from the Sun's surface. But the opposite is true. The solar atmosphere actually gets hotter. The temperature at the surface of the Sun is about 10,000°F (5,500°C). At the corona, the outermost part of the solar atmosphere, the average temperature can be more than 3,600,000°F (2,000,000°C).

Why is the corona so hot? No one knows for sure. That question has baffled scientists since 1942. That's when Swedish scientist Bengt Edlén discovered the corona's high temperature. Scientists think the temperature has something to do with the Sun's magnetic field.

The Sun's Magnetic Field

Magnets are common household items. You might use magnets to attach pictures to your refrigerator. Scientists imagine magnets as having a set of invisible lines around them. The set of lines around a magnet is called a magnetic field. The field is the region where magnetism, the force of the magnet, can be felt.

The Sun, Earth, and other objects have magnetic fields. The simplest magnetic fields consist of straight lines running smoothly from a magnet's north to south poles, or opposite ends. By comparison, the Sun's magnetic field is a mess. Instead of sweeping smoothly from pole to pole, the Sun's magnetic field twists and loops.

Like Earth, the Sun spins like a top. But because the Sun is not solid, it doesn't all turn at the same rate. At the Sun's equator, an imaginary line around its center, the Sun makes a complete circle once every twenty-five days. The Sun's north and south poles take thirty-five days to make a complete circle. In addition, the core of the Sun doesn't move at the same rate as the surface.

The different rates of speed twist up the Sun's magnetic field over time. As the magnetic field twists, patches of especially strong magnetism form and disappear. At these patches, magnetic field lines loop out of the Sun, then back in.

Magnets and *Magnetic Fields*

Every magnet has a magnetic field around it. The magnetic field is the magnet's zone of influence. Within the magnetic field, the force of the magnet can be felt. If you put two magnets near each other, you will feel them push or pull on one another. Their magnetic fields are interacting.

The magnetic field around a household magnet, such as a refrigerator magnet *(below)*, is simple. The field lines curve smoothly around the magnet. They run between the magnet's north and south poles.

Many objects in space, including stars and some planets, act like big magnets. They have magnetic fields around them. But the magnetic fields around these objects are rarely as simple as the magnetic field around a household magnet.

THE SUN'S MAGNETIC FIELD

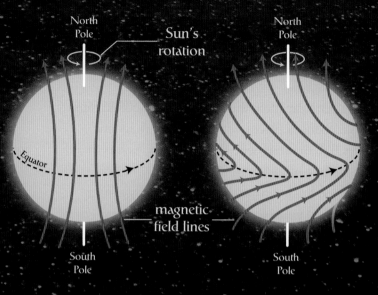

North Pole

Sun's rotation

Equator

magnetic field lines

South Pole

North Pole

South Pole

North Pole

South Pole

The Sun's untwisted magnetic field

Over time, the Sun's rotation distorts the magnetic field.

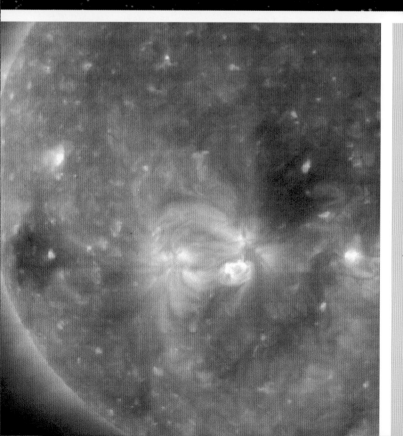

Above: *As the Sun spins, its magnetic field gets twisted over time.*

Left: *The Sun's magnetic field lines act like pathways for streams of plasma. In this image of the Sun, plasma streams follow field lines that loop from sunspot to sunspot (the white patches). The image is green because it was made using a special camera.*

Sunspots form at these loops. Sunspots are dark, cool patches on the Sun's surface. As the loops come and go, so do the sunspots.

Every nine to fourteen years, sunspot production peaks. The Sun's magnetic field is as twisted as it will get. We call this peak solar maximum, or solar max for short. After solar max, the Sun's magnetic field flips over. The Sun's south magnetic pole changes places with the north magnetic pole and vice versa. Along with this flip, the magnetic field untwists. Loops in the field disappear. The sunspot cycle begins again.

During all this activity, the magnetic field constantly transfers energy from the Sun's interior to its atmosphere. Have you ever snapped a towel like a whip? When you do this, energy travels from your hand to the tip of the towel. Scientists think waves in the Sun's magnetic field might carry energy out to the

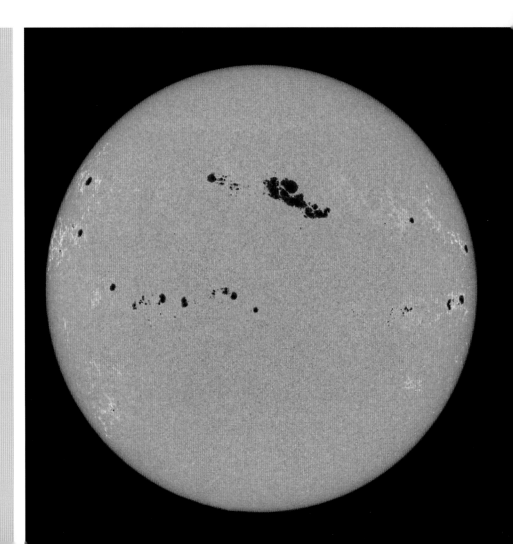

The dark areas in this image are sunspots. Sunspots appear darker in color because they are cooler than the surrounding regions.

> "The face [surface] of the sun is not without expression, but it tells us precious little of what is in its heart [core]."
>
> —U.S. astronomer Armin J. Deutsch, 1948

corona in the same way. The waves might "whip" atoms in the corona up to incredible temperatures. Scientists call this process wave heating.

Another possibility is that the untwisting and untangling of the Sun's magnetic field heats up the corona. When you twist up a rubber band, you are storing energy. If you let go of the rubber band, it quickly untwists. All the energy you stored powers the untwisting motion. Scientists think that the Sun's corona might get its energy in a similar way. The little twists and tangles in the Sun's magnetic field store energy. Each time the field untwists a little, some energy is released. Scientists call these little blasts of energy nanoflares. They may be the source of the corona's superheat.

2 Black Holes

This artist's illustration shows a supermassive black hole at the center of a galaxy.

ONE DAY, MORE THAN FIVE BILLION YEARS IN THE FUTURE, THE SUN WILL QUIT MAKING SUNSHINE. ITS CORE WILL RUN OUT OF THE HYDROGEN AND OTHER FUEL NEEDED FOR FUSION. WHEN FUSION STOPS, SO WILL THE OUTWARD RUSH OF LIGHT AND HEAT FROM THE SUN. NO OUTWARD FORCE WILL REMAIN TO FIGHT AGAINST THE INWARD PULL OF GRAVITY. GRAVITY WILL SQUEEZE THE ATOMS IN THE SUN'S CORE TIGHTER THAN EVER BEFORE. THE SUN WILL COLLAPSE. INSTEAD OF BEING FIFTY-FIVE TIMES WIDER THAN EARTH, THE CORE WILL BE NO WIDER THAN OUR PLANET. THE REST OF THE SUN WILL DRIFT AWAY IN SPACE.

After the Sun runs out of fuel, it will shrink and grow dim. This illustration shows the Sun glowing weakly above a darkened Earth.

When the Sun dies billions of years in the future, its core will become a type of star called a white dwarf. The white ball at the center of this image is a white dwarf.

The Sun's core will become a star called a white dwarf. At first, the white dwarf will give off light and heat. But eventually, its light and heat will fade. Over billions of years, it will become cold and dark.

DENSE AND DENSER

When a star larger than the Sun dies, its core's collapse is even more complete. Not only does gravity squeeze atoms tightly against other atoms, it actually crushes the atoms. Electrons smash against protons. They combine to make neutrons. The core becomes a neutron star.

Neutron stars contain more matter than the Sun, but they cram it all into a ball about 12 miles (19 kilometers) wide. With so much matter crammed into such a small space, a neutron star is heavy beyond belief. A golf-ball-sized piece of a neutron star would weigh more than 1 billion tons (0.9 billion metric tons) on Earth. That's heavier than the total weight of all the people on Earth.

As dense as a neutron star is, it's not as dense as matter can be. When the largest stars in the universe die, even neutrons do not survive. Gravity slams the collapsing matter together so violently that it is completely destroyed. What used to be the core of a giant star becomes a black hole.

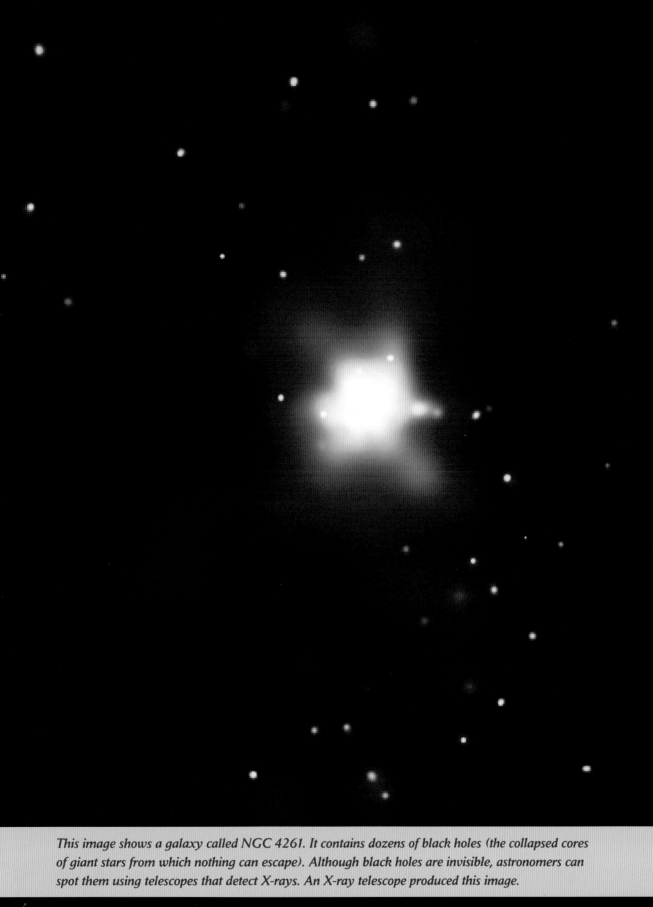

This image shows a galaxy called NGC 4261. It contains dozens of black holes (the collapsed cores of giant stars from which nothing can escape). Although black holes are invisible, astronomers can spot them using telescopes that detect X-rays. An X-ray telescope produced this image.

WARPING SPACE AND TIME

A black hole isn't an object because it isn't made of matter. A black hole is a point. At that point, space and time are a mess. They are stretched and distorted beyond our ability to recognize them. To understand what this means, we need to understand what space and time really are.

We live in four dimensions, or measures of space and time. Three of them—length, width, and height—are space dimensions. We measure distances in these dimensions. The fourth dimension is time. With these four dimensions, people can measure the where, how big, and when of any object. For instance, a pretzel can be on the floor 5 feet (1.5 m) east of, 3 feet (0.9 m) north of, and 2 feet (0.6 m) below you at four in the afternoon. We know its position in all four dimensions.

Because rulers are always the same size and clocks always tick at the same rate, we think of the four dimensions as rigid and unchanging. The truth is that space and time are stretchy. A foot (0.3 m) here is not necessarily the same as a foot there. One minute of time is not the same everywhere in the universe. Space and time can be warped.

Empty space—space with absolutely nothing in it—is smooth. If you throw in an object, the object warps the space around it just by being there. The more mass the object has, the more space stretches. Imagine a trampoline. It stays flat until you put something on it. If you throw a bowling ball onto the trampoline, the surface will sag downward. A person on the trampoline will make it sag even more.

Space is stretchy, just like the surface of a trampoline. If an elephant were to jump on this trampoline, imagine how much it would stretch.

It's A
Fact

The place inside a black hole where density is highest and space and time are the most warped is called a singularity.

Imagine you put an elephant on a trampoline. Elephants are so heavy that the trampoline would sag a long way. Because elephants are big, all that stretching would be spread over a big area of the trampoline. Then imagine the elephant started shrinking without changing its weight. Since the weight on the trampoline would stay the same, the amount of sagging would not change. But the elephant would touch less and less of the trampoline's surface as it shrank. Imagine the elephant shrank down to the size of a marble. All its weight would be concentrated in a very small space. At that spot, the trampoline would be stretched to the maximum.

That's what happens to space when a massive (containing a lot of mass) star collapses to become a black hole. All that mass shrinks down to a tiny dot. As it does, space gets stretched to the limit. Ultimately, the matter crunches down to nothing. All that is left is warped space.

Now for the really crazy part: black holes don't just stretch space. They stretch time too. A minute near a black hole is not the same as a minute on Earth. It's longer. Imagine a pair of twins with identical watches. Synchronize the watches so they tick in time with one another. Then send one of the twins toward a black hole. The twin falling toward the hole would see his or her watch tick normally the whole way down. But if you could compare the watches, you would see the falling twin's watch ticking more slowly than the watch that stayed outside the black hole. Now pretend you are somehow able to pull the falling twin back from the black hole. When you bring the twins back together, you'll find they aren't the same age anymore. The one who went to the black hole is younger. Time didn't pass as fast for that twin.

If one of these twins fell toward a black hole and was able to return, he would be younger than his sibling. Time doesn't move as quickly near a black hole as it does on Earth.

The Event Horizon

Measuring the size of a black hole is difficult. Because the matter that collapses to make a black hole is destroyed, there's nothing left to measure. Instead, scientists measure the distance around a black hole within which nothing can escape. This distance is called the event horizon. Any object within the event horizon is doomed. It ultimately will fall into the black hole and be destroyed. The event horizon of an ordinary black hole is about 19 miles (30 km) wide. But the stronger the black hole's gravity, the wider the event horizon will be.

The event horizon is the point of no return for something entering a black hole. Once beyond the horizon, there is no chance of escape.

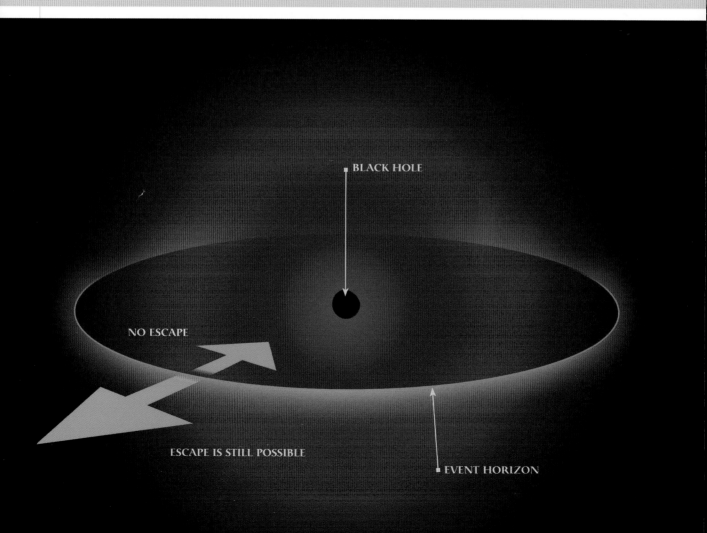

BLACK HOLE

NO ESCAPE

ESCAPE IS STILL POSSIBLE

EVENT HORIZON

IT'S A *Fact*

The speed of light is just over 670 million miles (1,078 km) per hour.

If more matter, such as a nearby star or planet, falls into a black hole, its event horizon will grow.

People sometimes imagine black holes to be predators, or hunters, gobbling up anything near them. But this is not the case. They exert no more gravity than the stars that collapsed to make them. Only objects within the event horizon are swallowed up.

Black holes are black because they give off no light. That's because not even light can escape from inside the event horizon of a black hole. To escape, an object would have to be moving faster than light can travel. Scientists think nothing can travel faster than light. So if light can't do it, neither can anything else.

Material falling toward a black hole does give off light. This material gets extremely hot and gives off high-intensity X-rays, a kind of energy. That's one way astronomers can find black holes. They look for places in space with a bright X-ray glow.

THE BIGGEST HOLES OF ALL

Black holes made from the collapse of a single star are called stellar black holes. Stellar black holes are incredibly powerful. They exert a grip that nothing can escape. But as strong as they are, stellar black holes are small. As it turns out, black holes come much bigger than that.

A stellar black hole may contain the mass of three to twenty Suns. But imagine a black hole with the pull of millions or even billions of Suns. This is called a supermassive black hole. Supermassive black holes are pretty common. Every galaxy in the universe may have a supermassive black hole at its center.

"Black holes are a major player in the evolution of the things that light up our night sky. They are, in a sense, the secret shadows behind the waltz of the galaxies."

—*U.S. astrophysicist Gregory Benford, 2006*

Galaxies are collections of millions, billions, or even trillions of stars. Some galaxies are shaped like soccer balls or footballs. Some are shaped like Frisbees. Some, such as our own Milky Way Galaxy are spiral shaped. No matter what their shape, all galaxies are held together by gravity. And at their centers, providing much of the necessary pull, are supermassive black holes.

Our galaxy, the Milky Way, is no exception. In the middle of the Milky Way is a black hole containing the mass of four million Suns. Everything in the galaxy spirals around it.

In this illustration, a black hole swallows up the remains of a nearby star.

MICRO BLACK HOLES!
Is Earth in Danger?

We know black holes can be stellar or supermassive. But some scientists think black holes also may come in size extra-small. They think some black holes are smaller than atoms. According to this idea, micro (extremely tiny) black holes form from the collision of subatomic particles (particles smaller than atoms) at very high speeds.

A device that can test these ideas is up and running. It's called the Large Hadron Collider (LHC), and it's in Switzerland. Scientists use the LHC to crash particles into one another at high speeds and see what happens.

Some people worry that the LHC could make micro black holes that could destroy Earth. But people needn't worry. Any micro black holes formed would last for only a tiny fraction of a second. They wouldn't have time to suck anything in before they vanished.

If we were in danger from micro black holes, we would already know it. High-speed particles collide all the time in nature. If those collisions do make micro black holes, they don't appear to be dangerous.

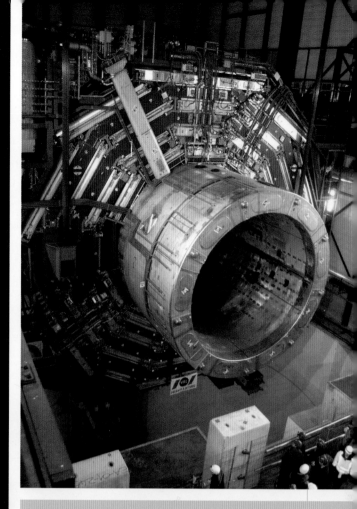

The Large Hadron Collider in Switzerland can smash particles together at high speeds. Some scientists think these collisions might create tiny black holes.

SPAGHETTIFICATION

What would happen if you fell into a black hole? In short, you would die. Anything falling past the event horizon of a black hole will be destroyed. Unfortunately for science-fiction lovers, you can't pass through a black hole into another universe. You can't use black holes for time travel either. But until certain death occurs, it would be a very interesting ride.

Falling toward a stellar black hole would feel pretty normal for a while. You would move faster and faster. Not much else would seem to change. But time would be slowing down. To you, your watch would appear to tick normally. But compared to time on the outside, each second would take longer and longer.

Eventually, you would start to feel the pull, and it wouldn't feel pleasant. Imagine you were falling in feet first. Your feet would be slightly closer to the singularity—the center of the black hole—than your head. This would make the pull of gravity on your feet greater than the pull on your head. Your feet would be pulled down faster. The black hole would begin to stretch you apart. At the same time, the space around you would get thinner and thinner. Your body would become the shape of spaghetti. Some call this process spaghettification.

An enormous disk of dust encircles a black hole in the center of galaxy NGC 7052 as shown in an artist's illustration. In several billion years, the black hole will entirely swallow the disk.

> "Black holes are laboratories for the most extreme conditions encountered in the . . . universe. Understanding black holes is crucial to understanding the universe. They are much more than an oddity found in galaxies."
>
> —U.S. astrophysicist Mitchell Begelman, 2003

As spaghettification increased, every cell of your body would be pulled apart. Your temperature would increase. Just outside the singularity, your matter would meet the inner horizon. The inner horizon is a violent mess of space and time. It's like the churning confusion at the bottom of a huge waterfall, only much hotter. Any of your matter that made it intact to the inner horizon would be ripped apart.

This scenario is based upon math and speculation, or educated guesses. Someday, humans might send a space probe into a black hole to see if all this speculation is correct. The probe could radio information back to Earth as it fell in. The problem is, once the probe got past the event horizon, we'd never hear another thing from it. Not even light can escape from a black hole, so any information the probe sent to us would be trapped as well. The mystery would remain.

3 A Universe WITH A BEGINNING

This illustration shows what the big bang—or beginning of the universe—might have looked like. In an instant, matter and energy rushed out from a tiny central point.

*H*AVE YOU EVER LOOKED AT THE NIGHT SKY AND JUST STARED INTO SPACE? NOT AT THE MOON, THE STARS, OR THE PLANETS, BUT THE BLACKNESS IN BETWEEN? PICK ANY PATCH OF DARK SKY. LET YOUR EYES ADJUST TO THE DARKNESS. IF YOU WAIT LONG ENOUGH, YOU WILL BEGIN TO SEE THAT THE EMPTY PATCHES AREN'T REALLY SO EMPTY. DIM LIGHTS—THE GLOW OF DISTANT OBJECTS—WILL APPEAR IN WHAT ORIGINALLY LOOKED JUST BLACK. BUT BETWEEN THOSE DIM LIGHTS, YOU WILL SEE MORE DARKNESS.

When people look at the night sky, they naturally wonder: How big is the universe? Does it go on forever? When did it begin?

The darkness raises some basic questions about our universe. How far does space extend? Is our universe infinite, or endless? Has our universe always been here? If not, how old is it and where did it come from?

GETTING A PICTURE OF THE UNIVERSE

First impressions are not always correct. In ancient times, people thought Earth was the center of the universe. They thought the Sun, the Moon, and the stars all traveled around Earth. In Alexandria, Egypt, a scientist named Ptolemy wrote about this idea in the A.D. 100s.

But scientists eventually learned more about space. In the 1500s, Polish astronomer Nicolaus Copernicus made detailed observations of the Sun and the planets. He used mathematics to show that Earth and other planets orbit, or travel around, the Sun. Copernicus wrote about his findings in a book called *On the Revolutions of the Heavenly Spheres.*

About seventy years later, Italian astronomer Galileo Galilei confirmed that Copernicus was right. Galileo used a new invention called a telescope. It made objects in the sky appear bigger. Telescopes allowed people to see that the universe was not what they had imagined.

Above: *In the 1500s, Nicolaus Copernicus figured out that Earth and the other planets orbited the Sun.* Below: *Galileo Galilei was the first person to use a telescope to study the sky, and he saw that Copernicus was correct.*

"The strongest affection and utmost zeal should, I think, promote the studies concerned with the most beautiful objects. This is the discipline that deals with the . . . stars' motions, sizes, distances, risings and settings . . . for what is more beautiful than heaven?"

—*Polish astronomer Nicolaus Copernicus, 1543*

In 1912, using a telescope much bigger than Galileo's, U.S. astronomer Vesto Slipher studied strange blobs called spiral nebulae. Astronomers thought they were gas clouds in our own Milky Way Galaxy. Slipher found that the spiral nebulae were moving faster than any star ever observed in our galaxy.

In the 1920s, U.S. astronomer Edwin Hubble also looked at spiral nebulae. He saw individual stars inside the nebulae. He determined that the stars couldn't be part of our own galaxy because they were too far away. For example, the spiral nebula Andromeda turned out to be more than 2 million

In the 1920s, astronomer Edwin Hubble realized that Andromeda (below) was a separate galaxy, not part of the Milky Way. He determined that the universe contains billions of galaxies.

IT'S A
Fact

A gas cloud in space is called a nebula. The plural of *nebula* is *nebulae* or *nebulas*.

light-years away. (A light-year is the distance light travels in one year.) Since our galaxy is only 100,000 light-years across, Andromeda could not be within our galaxy.

Hubble realized that the spiral blobs were not nebulae at all. They were entire galaxies. Hubble had discovered that our Milky Way was just one of many galaxies. Scientists had imagined a universe consisting of billions of stars. Instead, they realized that the universe contains billions of galaxies, each

What Is a *Light-Year?*

The distance light can travel through space in one year is called a light-year. One light-year is about 5.88 trillion miles (9.46 trillion km). Scientists use this distance like a measuring stick to describe how far apart objects are in space. For instance, the star Betelgeuse is about 640 light-years from Earth. That means it takes light about 640 years to travel from the star to us.

We can't see the entire Milky Way from Earth, because Earth is part of the Milky Way. This artist's illustration shows what the galaxy might look like.

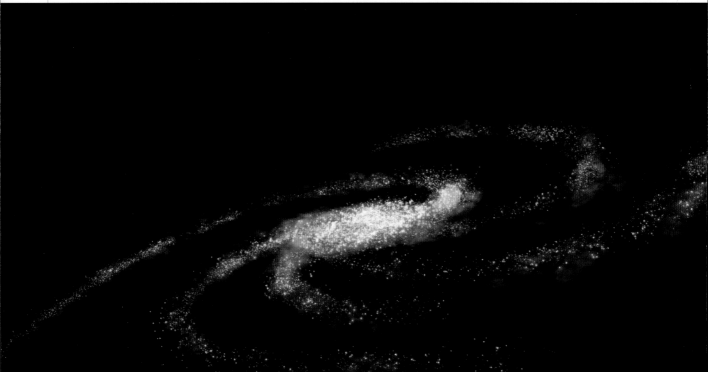

WITNESSING
the Past

Light is fast. Scientists think it can move through space faster than anything else. But as fast as it is, light still takes time to get places. It takes about 1.3 seconds for light to get from the Moon to Earth. Light takes about 8.3 minutes to travel to Earth from the Sun. It takes thousands of years to travel to us from many stars we see in the night sky.

Because light takes time to travel, we never see what anything in space looks like right now. For instance, when you look at the Sun, you see it as it was 8.3 minutes before. When you look at other stars, you see what they looked like when the light left them. You might see stars in the sky tonight that don't exist anymore. They may have blown up thousands of years ago. One day the light from the explosions will finally reach us. Only then will we know they happened.

When you look into space through a telescope, you actually are witnessing the past. The farther away in space you look, the farther back in time you will see. With very powerful telescopes, astronomers can actually observe things as they were soon after the universe was created.

containing billions of stars. The universe was bigger than people had originally thought.

Hubble studied Slipher's data. He also collected a lot of his own. When he put it all together, Hubble noticed that almost all galaxies were moving away from us. Hubble also realized that the farther from us the galaxies were, the faster they were moving away. He wrote about his findings in 1929.

Hubble's findings were nothing short of revolutionary. If galaxies are moving away from one another, they once were closer together. Prior to Hubble's work, many scientists thought the structure of the universe did not change. Hubble showed that the universe was expanding.

In your mind, you can rewind the expansion of the universe. That is, you can imagine everything moving toward one another instead of expanding. But you can rewind only so far back before everything is in one place. That place is the starting point of the universe. Prior to Hubble's evidence, many scientists thought the universe had always existed. Hubble's work showed that that couldn't be true. It showed that the universe had a beginning.

> *"From our home on the Earth, we look into the distances and strive to imagine the sort of world into which we are born. . . . The search will continue. The urge is older than history. It is not satisfied and it will not be suppressed."*
>
> —*U.S. astronomer Edwin Hubble, 1953*

THE BIG BANG UNIVERSE

By the early 1930s, using discoveries made by Hubble, Albert Einstein, and others, astronomers had devised a new theory about our universe. We call it the big bang model. The big bang model says that the space and time we live in have not always existed. According to the theory, they were created in an instant. Starting from a point of infinite density and unimaginable energy, the universe pushed outward. Space and time have been expanding ever since.

To many scientists of the time, the big bang theory seemed ridiculous. They strongly believed the universe had always existed. They would not accept the idea of it having a beginning. Even Albert Einstein thought the idea

Edwin Hubble studies the stars through a big telescope in the 1930s. He determined that the universe was expanding.

of an expanding universe was absurd at first, even though his own theories supported it. The scientists who backed the theory needed more evidence of a big bang.

SUCCESSFUL PREDICTIONS

Scientists realized that if the big bang model were true, our universe should be made primarily of the two most basic elements (types of atoms), hydrogen and helium. Those would have been the elements created during the big bang. Specifically, the big bang model says that about 75 percent of the atoms in our universe should be hydrogen and about 24 percent should be helium. The model says that other elements should make up no more than 1 percent of the universe. These amounts are exactly what scientists have found. Discovering these elements in these amounts led many more scientists to accept the big bang model. But some remained unconvinced. They wanted even more proof.

According to the big bang model, in the beginning, all energy in the universe was concentrated in a tiny space. This tiny space was incredibly hot. As space expanded, the energy spread out too. If the big bang theory were correct, every part of space would still glow a little bit from the big bang. Instead of visible light, the glow would take the form of low-energy microwaves. If scientists could find this glow, they would have strong evidence that the big bang actually happened.

In 1964 U.S. physicists Robert Wilson and Arno Penzias found the microwave glow. Astronomers call the glow the cosmic background radiation (CBR). Astronomers have carefully studied the CBR. They have found that outer space has exactly the level of energy we would expect to find if the big bang model is correct. In the twenty-first century, almost all astronomers agree that our universe began with a hot big bang.

THE ELECTROMAGNETIC *Spectrum*

If you pass white light through a prism—a triangular block of glass—it splits the white light into the colors of the rainbow: red, orange, yellow, green, blue, indigo (deep blue), and violet. The range of colors we see is called a spectrum.

The colors represent all the light we can see, but they don't represent all the light in the universe. It turns out that most types of light are invisible to us. They are always passing by you. Even when you're sitting in a perfectly dark room, you are surrounded by light. All matter in the universe gives off light. Stars and lightbulbs do, of course. But even objects that seem dark shine some kind of light.

Light travels in waves. Different kinds of light have different frequencies. Frequency is a measure of how many times something happens per second. The frequency of each kind of light depends on how many light waves travel past a certain point each second. The whole range of light frequencies in the universe is called the electromagnetic spectrum.

The light we can see is in the middle of this spectrum. Invisible light is found at each end of the spectrum. Infrared radiation, microwaves, and radio waves all have lower frequencies than visible light. Ultraviolet (UV) rays, X-rays, and gamma rays have higher frequencies than visible light.

The type of light an object gives off depends upon its temperature. The hottest objects in the universe shine gamma rays. The coldest ones emit only radio and microwaves.

Visible light—white light and the colors of the rainbow—is not the only light in the universe. Invisible light includes microwaves, radio waves, X-rays, and gamma rays.

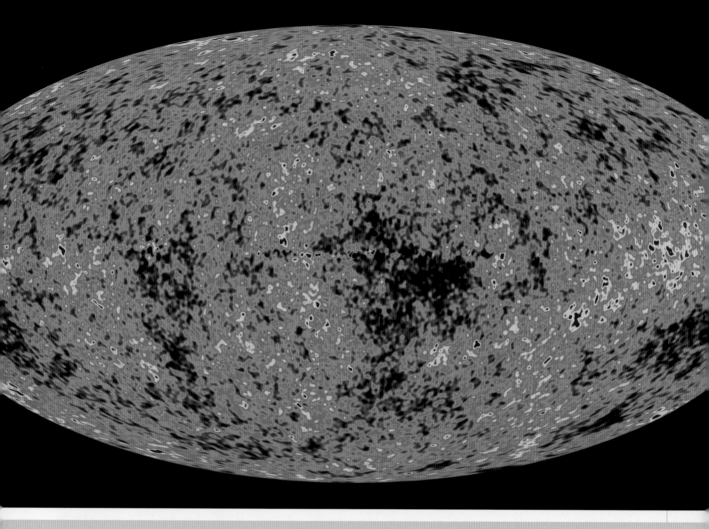

The discovery of the cosmic background radiation, shown on this map of the sky, provided more proof that the big bang theory was correct.

LOOKING BACKWARD

How old is our universe? To figure this out, scientists studied how quickly the universe is expanding. Based on this rate, astronomers then used mathematics to work backward. They determined how long it has been since everything in the universe was all in one place. That figure gives us the age of the universe. According to their calculations, it is about 13.7 billion years old.

IT'S A *Fact*

A scientist who studies the structure and history of the universe is called a cosmologist.

4 DARK Matter

A mysterious dark matter seems to be everywhere in the universe.

$\mathcal{H}$AVE YOU EVER SAT ON A SPINNING CHAIR? YOUR BODY FLIES OUTWARD AS THE CHAIR SPINS. THE FASTER THE CHAIR SPINS, THE HARDER IT IS TO STAY ON. YOU HAVE TO HOLD ON WITH GREATER FORCE. THE SAME IS TRUE IF YOU SWING AN OBJECT AROUND ON A STRING. THE FASTER YOU SWING IT, THE TIGHTER YOUR GRIP ON THE STRING MUST BE.

The Milky Way and other galaxies spin around, much like a spinning playground ride. Gravity keeps the stars inside galaxies from flying out into space.

Our galaxy, the Milky Way, is a big, spinning disk of stars. Gravity holds the galaxy together. Without enough gravity, stars would fly out of the galaxy as it turned. Stars aren't flying away, so gravity's grip must be tight enough.

The problem is that the numbers don't add up. Scientists have added up the mass of all the visible matter in the galaxy. They have figured out how much gravity all that stuff should exert on everything else. It turns out that gravity's grip seems too weak. The Milky Way's stars are traveling too fast to be held in by only the gravity of visible matter.

Our galaxy is not the only one with a gravity problem. None of the galaxies scientists have studied seem to have enough matter to hold themselves together.

*Like other galaxies, NGC 1672 (below) **doesn't seem to have enough matter to hold itself together. Is invisible "dark matter" at work in the universe?***

Gravity doesn't work only within galaxies. It works between galaxies as well. Many galaxies are a part of clusters, or groups. Galaxies move around within their clusters, but they always stay in the clusters. Clusters have the same gravity problems as individual galaxies. Clusters don't have enough visible matter to hold them together, but they do stay together.

THE MYSTERY OF THE DARK MATTER

When scientists discovered this mystery, they realized they must be missing something. The universe must have more matter than we know about—a lot more. And the extra matter must be difficult—or even impossible—to see.

The first person to suggest that "dark matter" exists was Swiss astronomer Fritz Zwicky, who wrote about it in 1933. At first, scientists thought dark matter might be in stars that are too cold and too dim for us to see. Perhaps dark matter was in black holes or neutron stars. Both are dark places that exert large gravitational pulls. Maybe dark matter was gas floating in space between stars. Maybe it was in undiscovered planets. However, none of these options can account for all the dark matter. They just don't have enough mass to solve the problem.

Modern scientists are coming to a startling conclusion. Whatever the dark matter is, it isn't the kind of matter we're used to. It can't be the kind that makes up stars or planets or people. It can't be ordinary matter.

Swiss astronomer Fritz Zwicky first wrote about the possibility of dark matter in 1933.

MATTER OF A DIFFERENT KIND

Ordinary matter is made of atoms and the particles inside them. These particles are protons, electrons, and neutrons. Protons and neutrons are made up of even smaller particles called quarks. But these are not the only kinds of particles in the universe. Scientists have discovered hundreds of other types.

To find new particles, scientists crash protons and other particles together at high speeds. When these particles collide, they break apart into smaller particles. Some of these small particles last on their own for only an instant before they combine with something else. Some small particles meet and destroy one another. Others fly away and are never seen again. Scientists think that one of these particles might be dark matter.

One such particle is the neutrino. Neutrinos are very tiny. They have almost no mass. They travel at nearly the speed of light. This speed makes it very hard for a clump of neutrinos to stay together. That means that neutrinos are probably not dark matter. If dark matter is good at anything, it's good at staying together.

WIMPs and axions are other candidates for dark matter. WIMP stands for weakly interacting, massive particles. WIMPs are heavy. One WIMP has more mass than one hundred protons. And WIMPS are slow. Unlike neutrinos, WIMPs will stay together in clumps. Axions are tiny like neutrinos, but they don't move as fast. They don't have as much trouble staying together as neutrinos do.

MACHOs

Some scientists think that dark objects such as black holes, neutron stars, and brown dwarfs (stars that don't get hot enough for fusion to begin) might account for dark matter. They might be found in a cloud surrounding galaxies. They might supply some of the extra gravity galaxies need to stay together. Scientists call these objects *massive compact halo objects*, or MACHOs. But MACHOs don't appear to be the best solution to the dark matter problem. They may account for some dark matter, but probably not most of it. Despite their name, WIMPs are a stronger possibility.

"[The discovery of dark matter would prove that] not only are we not at the center of the universe as we know it, but we aren't even made up of the same stuff as most of the universe."

—French physicist Bernard Sadoulet, 1992

In this illustration of the universe, gray circles represent dark matter. The red circles represent ordinary matter.

The problem with WIMPs and axions is that no one is absolutely sure they are real. Scientists have only predicted that they exist, although some scientists think they have detected WIMPs. Scientists are excited that these particles might be the dark matter everyone's been looking for. But until somebody finds these particles for sure, it's too early to celebrate.

Bottom left: *This machine is a neutrino accelerator. Scientists use it to fire neutrinos at high speeds to see what happens when neutrinos run into other particles.*
Bottom right: *This illustration shows a WIMP detector deep under Earth's surface. Are neutrinos or WIMPs the dark matter sought by scientists? No one yet knows.*

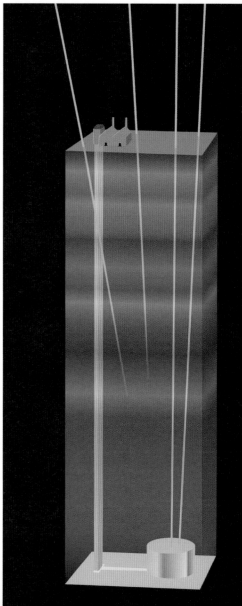

DETECTING DARK MATTER *Particles*

Because they are so small, neutrinos, WIMPs, and axions almost never run into anything. Neutrinos are flying through you right now. In fact, they can pass right through Earth and never strike another particle. And if WIMPs and axions exist, they do the same thing. Particles that almost never hit anything are very hard to detect. But once in a while, one of them should run into something. Each collision would generate a tiny amount of heat. A very sensitive detector might be able to spot that extra heat. With this in mind, scientists are building detectors around the world. The detectors are deep underground. One is in Antarctica, the continent that surrounds the South Pole. The detector is almost 1 mile (1.6 km) under ice.

A UNIVERSE FULL OF DARK MATTER

Science books say that the Milky Way is shaped like a spiral disk. The books say that the galaxy is about 100,000 light-years across. That accurately describes the visible part of our galaxy. But research into dark matter shows that we might be missing most of the picture. The shape of our galaxy might be more like a ball than a disk. The galaxy might be a ball of dark matter with a visible disk in the middle. It might have five times more dark matter than visible matter. It seems that most of our galaxy is a total mystery.

The same is true for the rest of the universe. Dark matter may be the explanation for all the gravity problems scientists see. If it is, dark matter must make up about 80 percent of the mass in the universe. The visible matter we see in our telescopes may only be one-fifth of all there is. Picturing the invisible has opened our eyes to a universe of possibilities.

" [With the discovery of dark matter] in a very real sense, astronomy begins anew. The joy and fun of understanding the universe we bequeath [pass on] to our grandchildren——and to their grandchildren. With over 90% of the matter in the universe still to play with, even the sky will not be the limit."

—U.S. astronomer Vera Rubin, 1990

DARK *Energy*

Why is the universe expanding faster and faster? A force called dark energy might be the answer.

$\mathcal{W}$HEN YOU THROW A BALL STRAIGHT UP INTO THE AIR, IT BEGINS TO SLOW AS SOON AS IT LEAVES YOUR HAND. GRAVITY IS PULLING DOWNWARD ON THE BALL. EVENTUALLY, THE BALL WILL STOP MOVING UPWARD. THEN IT WILL START TO FALL. AS IT FALLS, IT WILL GAIN SPEED UNTIL IT LANDS BACK IN YOUR HAND.

Gravity will pull this ball back to the young man's hand. But in space, dark energy might work against gravity—pushing things away from one another.

What if you threw the ball up and, just like normal, it began to slow down. But what if instead of stopping and coming back, it started going upward faster. What if it just kept going upward and never came back? You would be perplexed. You might wonder if it had been carried up by some strange wind. You might even think your ball had been abducted by space aliens. But you definitely wouldn't think it was normal.

That's because when gravity is the only force working on the ball, it's going to come down. For the ball to race upward, another force must be working against the downward pull of gravity.

A STARTLING DISCOVERY

After the big bang, the universe expanded outward. All the matter that was created began to spread apart. Every piece of matter is attracted to every other piece of matter by gravity, so everything was pulling on everything else. If the outward expansion hadn't been fast enough, gravity would have pulled everything back together right away. But the expansion was fast, and everything kept moving outward.

But gravity never quits. Everything was still pulling on everything else. So even though the expansion of the universe continued, it began to slow down. With this in mind, scientists tried to measure how much the expansion was slowing down.

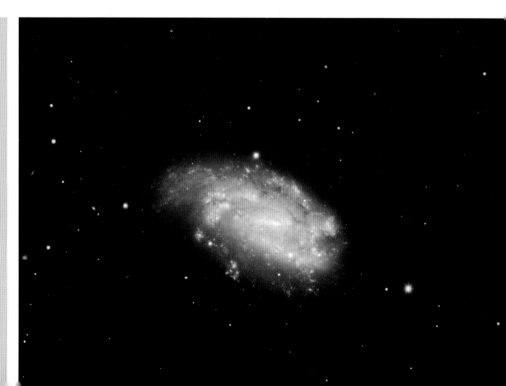

The bright dot directly above spiral galaxy NGC 1559 is a Type 1a supernova. All Type 1a supernovae have the same brightness. The dimmer they are, the farther away they are from Earth.

Type 1a Supernovae: *Standard Candles*

A supernova is an exploding star. A Type 1a supernova occurs when a white dwarf and a normal star orbit each other. The white dwarf's gravity draws matter from the regular star. The mass of the white dwarf grows. When the white dwarf's mass reaches a critical point, the white dwarf explodes. For a short time, Type 1a supernovae shine brighter than the light from an entire galaxy of normal stars. Because they all occur in the same way, all Type 1a supernovae have the same brightness. Astronomers call these supernovae standard candles. They help astronomers figure out how far away something is in space.

Imagine you looked through a telescope and saw two Type 1a supernovae. Imagine that one looked brighter than the other one. That would mean that the dimmer one was farther away. If they were the same distance away, they would look equally bright. The measure of brightness tells astronomers how far away a supernova is. Astronomers can measure the brightness of supernovae in distant galaxies to figure out how far away the galaxies are.

Using light from exploding stars called Type 1a supernovae, in the late 1990s, scientists calculated speeds for various galaxies. When they analyzed the data, they made a startling discovery. The universe was expanding faster than expected. In fact, the calculations showed that the universe was not slowing down at all. Its expansion was actually speeding up.

If gravity is the only force controlling the expansion of the universe, the expansion should slow down. For the universe to race outward, another force must be at work against the inward pull of gravity.

DARK ENERGY

What is causing the outward push? Scientists don't know, but they have given it a mysterious name. They call it dark energy. While gravity works to hold things together, dark energy pulls the universe apart.

Scientists think that after the big bang, gravity dominated for a while. The expansion of the universe slowed down. But as the universe grew, the influence of gravity lessened. When the universe got big enough, gravity could no longer dominate. The outward

IT'S A *Fact*

The idea that empty space might be full of particle activity comes from a branch of physics called quantum mechanics.

push of dark energy took over. The expansion of the universe speeded up. And it's been speeding up ever since.

The force of dark energy appears to come from empty space. Some scientists think something in space itself causes the outward push. Space looks empty, but it may not be as empty as it seems. Perhaps something is happening between tiny particles that we've never seen. Perhaps all that activity causes an outward push. Scientists admit that it's a wild idea, but no one has a more sensible explanation.

If dark energy comes from space, it makes sense that its influence should be increasing. Space has been expanding since the big bang. The more space there is, the bigger the push from dark energy.

It's possible that the calculations are wrong and that there is no outward push after all. Or maybe scientists don't really understand gravity. But most scientists think there is no mistake. The best evidence points toward dark energy—and a lot of it. If dark energy is real, it makes up most of the energy in the universe.

THE BIG CHILL

Scientists once imagined that we lived in a round-trip universe. They thought the universe would expand for a while, but then gravity would eventually win. The expansion of the universe would end, and everything would start coming back together. Faster and faster, the universe would contract until everything collapsed in a big crunch. End of universe.

"*The term [dark energy] doesn't mean anything. It might not be dark. It might not be energy. The whole name is a placeholder. It's a placeholder for the description that there's something funny that was discovered . . . that we don't understand.*"

—*U.S. astronomer David Schlegel, 2007*

If the universe stopped expanding and started shrinking, eventually, everything would come together in a big crunch. It might take the form of a big, bright flash, as shown in this illustration.

Dark energy changes that theory. A universe dominated by dark energy probably is on a one-way trip. If dark energy is everywhere, the universe will probably expand forever. No crunch. No end of the universe.

Avoiding the big crunch might sound like a good thing. But never-ending expansion wouldn't be pleasant either. Galaxies would spread farther and farther from us. Eventually they would be too far away to see. Material in the Milky Way that normally created stars would spread out. Eventually, it would spread too far for new stars to form. As old stars in our galaxy burned out, the night sky would get

If the universe expands endlessly, stars will burn out and no new stars will form. The universe will be cold, dark, and lifeless.

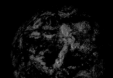

"We are incredibly lucky to be working just at the moment when the pieces of the cosmic [universe's] jigsaw puzzle are falling into place, locking together, and revealing the outline of the pieces yet to come. Dark energy is the biggest missing piece and a place where astronomical observations point to a gaping hole in the present knowledge of fundamental physics."

—U. S. astrophysicist Robert Kirshner, 2003

darker. All visible light would fade. In time our galaxy would become cold, dark, and almost totally alone in the universe.

This scenario assumes that dark energy will push forever outward. But we know almost nothing about dark energy. If dark energy changed over time, if it weakened or switched somehow, a big crunch would still be possible.

No matter what, there is no need to panic. Scientists who study dark matter don't expect anything to change soon. Whether it's heading for a big crunch or a big chill, the universe appears to have billions of good years ahead.

TRAVELING THROUGH
Space and Time

The Mars global surveyor took ten months to travel from Earth to Mars. Traveling to more distant planets or traveling beyond the solar system takes much longer.

$\mathcal{I}$N MOVIES AND ON TV, HUMANS ZIP FROM GALAXY TO GALAXY. THEY TRAVEL AT SPEEDS FASTER THAN LIGHT AND MAKE IT LOOK EASY. IN REAL LIFE, THOUGH, SPACE TRAVEL IS NOT SO SIMPLE. HUMANS HAVE NEVER BEEN ANY FARTHER FROM HOME THAN THE MOON. WE'VE SENT SPACE PROBES TO OTHER PLANETS, BUT FORGET ABOUT GETTING THEM THERE AT HYPERSPEED. OUR PROBES TAKE MONTHS TO GET TO EVEN THE CLOSEST PLANETS.

In the film and TV series Star Trek, *spaceships covered millions of miles in no time. The reality of space travel is much different.*

What about zipping from galaxy to galaxy? Will it be possible one day to jump in a spaceship, visit a distant galaxy, and be back before dinner? Maybe. But before we can do that, we have some problems to overcome.

THE DISTANCE PROBLEM

Let's say we could shrink the universe. In the real universe, Earth is about 93 million miles (150 million km) from the Sun. In our shrunken universe, let's say the distance between them is only the distance across a dime. That is, one dime represents 93 million miles (150 million km) of space. Using that scale, the dwarf planet Pluto would be about thirty-nine dimes away from us. At this scale, how far away would the nearest star be? How about the nearest galaxy beyond our own?

The nearest star to Earth (besides the Sun, of course) is Proxima Centauri. On the dime scale, you'd need $27,000 in dimes to reach Proxima Centauri. To reach Andromeda, the closest galaxy like our own, you'd need more than $15 billion in dimes. And those are just the closest. Other stars and galaxies

This small, glowing ball, photographed through the Chandra Space Telescope, is Proxima Centauri, the star closest to the Sun. Modern spacecraft would have to travel for tens of thousands of years to reach it.

It would take more than two million years to reach the Andromeda Galaxy (left)—even at the speed of light.

are even farther away. The point is this: *anywhere* we might want to go is tremendously far away. And traveling long distances takes lots of time.

THE SPEED PROBLEM

Light travels more than 670 million miles (1 billion km) per hour. Most scientists think that *nothing* can travel faster than light. No matter how powerful, a spaceship could never go faster than light. Light speed is the ultimate speed limit.

"I think the one overwhelming emotion that we had was when we saw the earth rising in the distance over the lunar landscape. . . . It makes us realize that we all do exist on one small globe, for from 230,000 miles [370,000 km] away it really is a small planet."

—Frank Borman, U.S. astronaut, 1969

This is a real problem for space travelers. Why? The speed limit is much too low. Even at light speed, most stars are farther away than a person could travel in a lifetime. And forget about going to other galaxies. It would take nearly one hundred thousand years to cross the visible part of our *own* galaxy at light speed. To get to the Andromeda Galaxy would take more than two million years. The bottom line is, for humans to travel to other stars or galaxies, we need a way to break the speed limit.

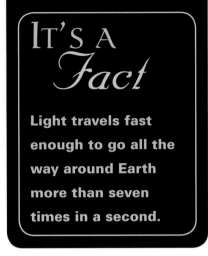

SHORTCUTS THROUGH SPACE

Space travel would be quicker if you didn't have to travel through all the space between two points. To understand how this might work, draw two dots on a sheet of paper. Make the dots as far away from each other as possible. Draw a line between the dots. To do that, you have to trace across all the space in between them. But if the paper was folded, you could poke your pencil through one of the dots to make a passageway to the other dot—a shortcut. You could go from dot to dot without ever having to trace across the rest of the paper.

Space may contain shortcuts like that. A place called a wormhole might be just the ticket. A wormhole is basically the mouths of two black holes connected by a tunnel. Einstein's theories about space and time predict that wormholes could exist. But where can you find one?

Think about a piece of fabric. From a distance, the fabric looks smooth and solid. But with a microscope, you can see that the fabric has lots of tiny holes in it. It's possible that space is kind of like fabric. The fabric of space may have tiny holes or tubes in it. These holes or tubes are wormholes. No one has ever seen one. They are much too small to see—far smaller than any particle that scientists have ever discovered. And if they are there, they don't stay around for long. They open and close quickly. Then a new one pops open in a different place.

If you could find a wormhole and stretch it open, you might be able to pass through it. The hole might allow you to travel quickly to faraway places in space. The hole might lead to another universe. Some scientists think you might even be able to use wormholes to time travel.

This artist's illustration shows a spaceship exiting a wormhole to reach a solar system far from our own.

Remember that time slows down for any object that falls into a black hole. According to Einstein's theories, the same thing happens when an object travels at very high speeds. The process is called time dilation. Time dilation actually happens at any speed. It happens to you when you travel fast in a car. You just don't notice it because the effect is so small. But near the speed of light, the effect of time dilation is huge.

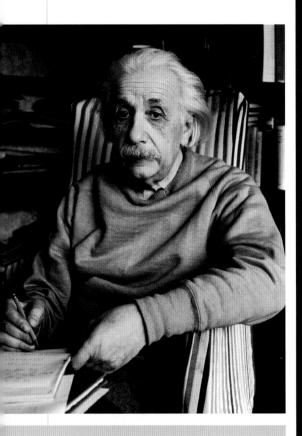

Albert Einstein, shown here in the 1940s, had a creative mind that revolutionized physics.

EINSTEIN: *A Revolutionary Mind*

Much of our understanding of space and time is based upon the work of German physicist Albert Einstein. Einstein did not merely build upon the ideas of scientists who came before him. He revolutionized our way of thinking about the universe.

Albert Einstein was born in Germany in 1879. As a boy, he did not like school. But he loved to think. He loved to read and study. After high school, he studied physics at a college in Switzerland.

Einstein's genius was in his ability to imagine. He imagined what it would be like to travel at the speed of light. He imagined how an event might look to two different people viewing it from different angles or at different speeds.

After college, Einstein became a clerk in a Swiss government office. The job gave him plenty of time to simply imagine. He studied and wrote papers about physics. In 1905 a German scientific journal published three of Einstein's articles. His writings explained how space, time, and the speed of light are related. The information was so valuable to science that 1905 is often called Einstein's *annus mirabilis*, which is Latin for "miracle year."

Einstein eventually became a college professor. He went on to publish more groundbreaking discoveries, including his general theory of relativity in 1915.

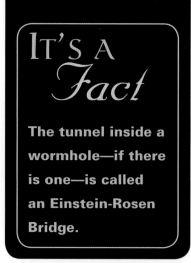

IT'S A
Fact

The tunnel inside a
wormhole—if there
is one—is called
an Einstein-Rosen
Bridge.

Imagine you could grab one mouth of a wormhole. Imagine you could send that mouth on a trip at nearly the speed of light. Time would slow down for that mouth. At the end of the trip, the mouth wouldn't just be in another place. It would be in another time. If you jump into the mouth, you would travel through the wormhole to another time—assuming you could hold the wormhole open long enough.

Unfortunately, keeping a wormhole open would be pretty hard. To do it, you would need something called exotic matter. Exotic matter would exert antigravity—an outward force that could hold the hole open. The problem is, as far as we know, exotic matter doesn't exist. So if we are going to break the speed limit, we probably shouldn't count on using shortcuts.

WARPING SPACE

Remember the dots? What if you drew your dots on a rubber sheet instead of paper? You could make the dots closer by stretching and squeezing the rubber sheet. What if space itself could be stretched or squeezed like a rubber sheet?

That's the idea behind hyperspace or warp drives. Imagine if your spaceship could actually shrink the space in front of it. You could travel great distances through space without having to go faster than light.

Warp drive is no more than an idea. But ideas are where revolutions in science begin. Someday long-distance space travel might be possible. In the meantime, people will have to settle for slow and steady.

"Nature has not given us hints about how to get to another star. It's difficult enough to travel within the solar system."
—*NASA astronomer and Nobel Prize winner John Mather, 2010*

7 Life BEYOND EARTH

Some planets, such as Gliese 581d (illustrated above), *may be similar to Earth. But does that mean they might hold life?*

$\mathcal{W}$E LIVE IN A UNIVERSE WITH THE RIGHT CONDITIONS FOR LIFE. TO CONFIRM THIS, ALL YOU HAVE TO DO IS LOOK IN THE MIRROR. LIFE MOST DEFINITELY EXISTS ON EARTH. BUT THAT DOESN'T MEAN LIFE IS EVERYWHERE IN THE UNIVERSE. IT DOESN'T EVEN GUARANTEE THAT LIFE IS ANYWHERE BEYOND EARTH.

This photo of Earth from space shows it is a planet of water, land, and atmosphere, making it suitable for life as we know it.

Are other planets capable of sustaining life? Where should we look? Does all life have to resemble life on Earth? If not, what might other life-forms be like? A new field of science is devoted to answering those questions. It's called astrobiology. (Biology is the study of life, and *astro* comes from the ancient Greek word for star.)

Biologists know a lot about life on Earth. They know that all life-forms on Earth contain lots of water. Water is essential to life on Earth, so water might be just as important to life in other places. For astrobiologists, places with water are natural starting points for the hunt for life beyond Earth.

FOLLOW THE WATER

The good news for those looking for life beyond Earth is that water is common. Our solar system is loaded with water. The bad news is that just having water is not enough. Water has to be in the right form for life to use it.

For life, water must be liquid. Almost every planet and moon in our solar system has water. But most of this water is not liquid. If the water is too close to the Sun, it evaporates, or turns into gas. If the water is too far away from the Sun, it freezes. It becomes ice. Earth is just the right distance away from the Sun for most of its water to remain liquid. Astrobiologists call this perfect distance the circumstellar habitable zone, which means the livable area around a star.

The only other body in the Sun's circumstellar habitable zone is the Moon. But the Moon has no atmosphere, or layer of gases around its surface. Earth's atmosphere acts like a blanket. It traps heat from the Sun. This heat keeps water from freezing. Without an atmosphere to trap the Sun's heat, water on the Moon freezes.

The surface of the planet Mars is dry and barren. But it wasn't always that way. Recent discoveries show that a few billion years ago, Mars was a very wet place. It had a thicker atmosphere, which held moisture and trapped heat from the Sun. Mars may have been habitable—suitable for life—at some point in the past. Perhaps life thrived there when the planet was still young, about four billion years ago.

"When you look at the stars and the galaxy, you feel you are not just from any particular piece of land, but from the solar system."

—*U.S. astronaut Kalpana Chawla, 2003*

Above: *Water in liquid form is vital for life.*

Below: *These channels, perhaps created by floodwaters, show that Mars may once have had liquid water on its surface.*

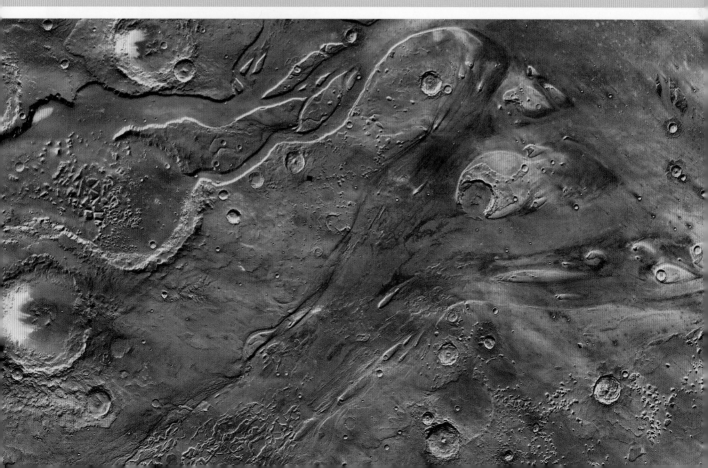

SUNLIGHT OPTIONAL

One way or another, most life on Earth gets its energy from the Sun. Plants make their own food using energy from sunlight. People and animals eat plants to get energy. People and some animals also eat animals. Whether stored in plants or animals, all this energy originally came from the Sun.

But not all life on Earth relies on sunlight. Some bacteria—tiny organisms— live deep underground. They live in caves and cracks in rocks that sunlight never reaches. Some bacteria live in the darkest parts of the ocean. These life-forms get energy from oil seeping from the ocean floor. Others get energy from deep-sea volcanoes, places where hot gases and melted rocks erupt from inside Earth.

Right: *The microscopic tardigrade, or water bear, can live in extreme cold and extreme heat.*
Below: *Other living things on Earth get their energy from underwater volcanoes. Perhaps life-forms have adapted to extreme conditions on other planets.*

Perhaps a liquid ocean lies beneath the ice of Europa, one of Jupiter's moons. And this ocean might be home to life.

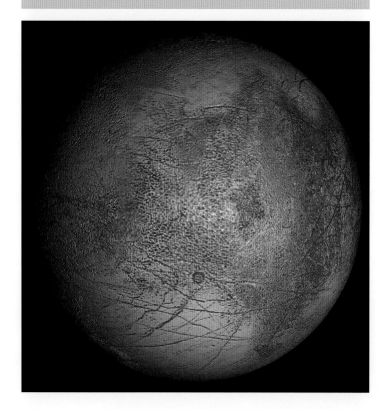

Since some life on Earth doesn't rely on sunlight, perhaps life beyond Earth doesn't need it either. It might survive on underground energy. Scientists think that Mars might have liquid water below its surface. If it does, life might exist underground on Mars.

The planet Jupiter has many moons. One of the largest is Europa. Europa is totally covered in ice. The temperature at its surface is −260°F (−162°C). But Europa might be warmer below the surface. It might contain a liquid ocean below the ice. Heat from inside the moon might keep the water from freezing. Astrobiologists say life might exist in this kind of underground environment. If so, the habitable zone of our solar system might be wider than we think.

FINDING EXOPLANETS

Just as the Sun has planets, other stars have planets too. Planets that orbit stars other than the Sun are called exoplanets. Some scientists look for Earthlike exoplanets that might support life.

Since discovering the first exoplanet in 1992, scientists have found hundreds more. But almost all the exoplanets are giant planets. They are even bigger than Jupiter and are made of gas. Almost all of them are very close to the stars they orbit, which makes them very hot. Astronomers call these planets hot Jupiters. Such hot, gassy planets are probably unsuitable for life as we know it. It's unlikely that anything could survive in such extreme environments.

Rocky, Earth-sized planets are more likely to hold life. Scientists discovered the first rocky exoplanet in 2005. To find more such planets, the U.S. National Aeronautics and Space Administration launched Kepler in March 2009. Kepler is a telescope that orbits Earth. Unlike Earth-based telescopes, Kepler doesn't have to look through Earth's thick atmosphere to view space. Kepler gets a clearer view of space than telescopes on the ground.

Kepler is designed to look for Earthlike exoplanets. Kepler has found some interesting planets. Some are close to the size of Earth. Some are rocky. Some have water and other chemicals needed for life on Earth. None of the planets are just like Earth, but scientists are still excited. They think that if we keep looking, we might find life on an exoplanet.

Along with Kepler, scientists use other ground- and space-based telescopes to search for exoplanets. NASA plans to launch two more missions in the 2010s. Both are new space telescopes. SIM Lite will look for habitable zones around stars. The Terrestrial Planet Finder will take pictures of exoplanets.

NASA technicians load fuel into Kepler in preparation for its 2009 launch. The space-based telescope searches for Earthlike planets.

This illustration shows the SIM Lite spacecraft moving through space looking for habitable zones around stars.

ENCOURAGING ODDS

Our galaxy is large. Very, very, very large. It contains about one hundred billion stars. That number is hard to imagine. But consider this. If you had one hundred billion pieces of popped popcorn, they would fill 160 Olympic-sized swimming pools.

Many of those one hundred billion stars probably have planets orbiting them. Some of those planets are rocky. Some have water. Some rocky planets most likely orbit within their star's habitable zone.

With numbers like these, the odds seem good that at least some other planets in our galaxy have the right conditions for life. Some planets might have only simple life-forms, such as bacteria. Others might be home to advanced, intelligent life-forms. They might be capable of communicating with us. Some scientists think the odds are good that many such planets exist.

Our galaxy is just one of many in the universe. Astronomers think the universe holds hundreds of billions of galaxies. Each galaxy contains millions or billions of stars. Therefore, planets in our universe may number in the trillions. If any galaxies are like ours, life might be all over the universe. Perhaps our universe is full of intelligent life.

To find out, a group of scientists started the SETI Institute in 1984. SETI stands for the *Search* for *Extraterrestrial Intelligence*. (*Extraterrestrial* means "beyond Earth.") SETI scientists use radio telescopes—telescopes tuned to receive radio waves—to search for signals from other planets. The scientists use powerful computers to try to decode any signals they receive. So far, SETI has not detected any signals from extraterrestrials. But scientists are confident that if they keep looking, one day they will.

COMPLICATING THE ODDS

Not all scientists are so optimistic. They say the odds may not be as good as they seem. The conditions for life might be harder to meet than we imagine.

Although our galaxy contains about one hundred billion stars, not all stars are the same. Most of the one hundred billion stars are red dwarfs. Red dwarfs are tiny, dim, and cold compared to the Sun. To get enough sunlight to support life, a planet might have to be very close to a red dwarf. Planets that are very close to a star often are unable to spin freely. Instead, one side of the planet always faces the star. That side is always scalding hot. The side facing away from the star is always extremely cold. Nowhere on the planet is the temperature bearable. Because of this, some scientists think planets that orbit red dwarfs are unlikely to have life.

Not all locations in our galaxy are the same either. In many areas within the Milky Way, stars are much closer together than they are in Earth's

GAMMA RAY *Bursts*

When a large star dies, its core collapses. The rest of the star explodes outward. The explosion showers any nearby planets with high-energy particles and radiation.

The largest exploding stars are called hypernovae. These are the most powerful explosions in the universe. Hypernovae emit gamma ray bursts (GRBs). GRBs release more energy per second than the brightest galaxy. The surface of any planet in the path of a GRB would be burned to a crisp. Some scientists think GRBs might limit the number of planets with intelligent life.

neighborhood. Levels of high-energy radiation, such as X-rays, are much greater in areas with close-together stars. Life in those places is much more likely to get roasted by dangerous radiation. Some scientists think that large parts of every galaxy in the universe may be too hazardous for life.

These factors lower the odds of extraterrestrial life considerably, but they still leave a lot of stars to choose from. Other factors may lower the odds further. A planet's size, the strength of its magnetic field, the makeup of its atmosphere, and many more factors may limit a planet's ability to host living organisms. In addition, natural disasters such as supernova explosions or asteroid (rocks in space) impacts could wipe out life on a perfectly good planet.

OTHER TYPES OF LIFE

All this talk of odds is based on an assumption. It's based upon the idea that life in our universe must be like life on Earth. But some scientists say we need to use more imagination. It's a big universe, and we know so little about it. Maybe life could take a form totally unlike anything on Earth. It might be made of other chemicals. It might use some other kind of energy. It might inhabit planets that Earth life-forms never could. It might take some form we've never suspected. We have so much to learn.

"We need to keep an open mind for possible [life]-signs in unexpected places as we explore the entire solar system and beyond. If we relax our (understandable) attachment to 'life as we know it,' other intriguing possibilities become worthy of our consideration."

—David Grinspoon, curator of astrobiology, Denver Museum of Nature and Science, 2002

TIMELINE

A.D. 100s Greek scientist and mathematician Ptolemy writes that Earth is the center of the universe.

1542: Polish astronomer Nicolaus Copernicus publishes *On the Revolutions of the Heavenly Spheres*, which argues that Earth and the planets orbit the Sun.

1609: Italian astronomer Galileo Galilei uses a telescope to study the night sky. He confirms Copernicus's idea that Earth and the planets orbit the Sun.

1905: German physicist Albert Einstein publishes his special theory of relativity, which explains how space, time, and the speed of light are related. The theory includes the famous equation $E = mc^2$.

1912: Vesto Slipher discovers that "spiral nebulae" (which scientists later learn are galaxies) are moving faster than any star ever observed in our galaxy.

1915: Albert Einstein publishes his general theory of relativity. The theory later helps scientists understand black holes and the big bang.

1929: U.S. astronomer Edwin Hubble publishes the idea that the farther away a galaxy is from us, the faster it is moving away from us. Astronomers use this idea to propose the big bang model.

1933: Swiss astronomer Fritz Zwicky first proposes the presence of dark matter in the universe.

1942: Swedish scientist Bengt Edlén discovers that the temperature of the Sun's corona is unexpectedly high.

1964: Physicists Robert Wilson and Arno Penzias discover cosmic background radiation, which is leftover energy from the big bang.

1984: Scientists start the SETI Institute to search for signals from extraterrestrial life.

1992: Scientists make the first discovery of an exoplanet—a planet outside our solar system.

late 1990s: Working independently, two teams of astronomers discover that the expansion of the universe is increasing, contrary to expectations. The discovery suggests the presence of "dark energy" everywhere in the universe.

2005: Scientists make the first discovery of a rocky exoplanet.

2009: The National Aeronautics and Space Administration launches Kepler to look for rocky exoplanets.

2010: Scientists encourage bacterium to live on arsenic, expanding the idea of what life can be in the universe.

2011: NASA and the U.S. Department of Energy launch the Joint Dark Energy Mission.

CHOOSE AN EIGHTH WONDER

Now that you've read *Seven Wonders of Space Phenomena*, do a little research to choose an eighth wonder. You may enjoy working with a friend. To start your research, look at some of the websites and books listed on the following pages. Use the Internet and library books to find more information. What other aspects of space are phenomenal? Think about things that

- *sound like science fiction*
- *are still mysteries to astronomers*
- *are extremely large or extremely small*

You might even try gathering photos and writing your own chapter on the eighth wonder.

GLOSSARY

astrobiology: the study of life in space

atmosphere: a layer of gas or plasma surrounding a body in space. The body's gravity holds the atmosphere in place.

atom: the particle considered to be the basic building block of matter

black hole: an invisible place in space where gravity is so strong that nothing can escape from it

dark energy: a mysterious force that seems to be working against the pull of gravity

dark matter: invisible matter that provides extra gravity within and between galaxies

density: the degree to which something is tightly packed together

element: a type or kind of atom. Oxygen, hydrogen and helium are examples of elements.

event horizon: the margin around a black hole within which nothing can escape

exoplanet: a planet that is not part of our solar system

frequency: a measure of how many times something happens per second. The frequency of light depends on how many light waves travel past a certain point per second.

galaxy: a group of millions, billions, or even trillions of stars, held together by gravity

gravity: a force of attraction that all matter exerts

light-year: the distance light can travel through space in a year (about 5.88 trillion miles, or 9.46 trillion km)

magnetic field: the zone around a magnet within which the magnet's force is exerted

mass: the amount of material or matter in an object

matter: physical stuff; all objects are made of matter

nebula: a cloud of gas and/or plasma in space

neutron star: the collapsed core of a star that is very large but not large enough to make a black hole

nuclear fusion: combining atoms to build bigger atoms

orbit: to travel around an object in space due to the pull of gravity; the path an object takes through space as it is pulled around another object

plasma: a state of matter formed by heating up gas

quarks: tiny particles that are the building blocks of protons and neutrons

singularity: the point at the very center of a black hole, where space and time are warped infinitely

white dwarf: the burned-out core of a small or medium star. White dwarfs are hot enough to shine white light but are not hot enough for fusion.

wormhole: a tunnel connecting two black holes

Source Notes

8 Curt Suplee, "The Sun: A Stormy Star," *National Geographic*, July 1, 2004, 4.

15 Armin J. Deutsch, "Eyes Turned Skyward," Spacequotations.com, 2008–2010, http://spacequotations.com/sunquotes.html (August 26, 2010).

23 Gregory Benford, "Monster of the Milky Way," *NOVA*, October 31, 2006, http://www.pbs.org/wgbh/nova/transcripts/3314_blackhol.html (August 26, 2010).

27 Daniel Kane, "The Dark Side of the Universe," msnbc.com, June 19, 2003, http://www.msnbc.msn.com/id/3077421/ns/technology_and_science-science (August 26, 2010).

31 Nicolaus Copernicus, "Eyes Turned Skyward," Spacequotations.com, 2008–2010, http://spacequotations.com/astronomyquotes.html (September 14, 2010).

34 Edwin Hubble, ibid.

42 John Noble Wilford, "Physicists Step Up Exotic Search for Universe's Missing Mass," *New York Times*, May 26, 1992, http://www.nytimes.com/1992/05/26/science/physicists-step-up-exotic-search-for-the-universe-s-missing-mass.html (August 26, 2010).

45 Katrina Thompson, "Vera Rubin's Dark Universe," Lake Afton Public Observatory, October 1990, http://webs.wichita.edu/lapo/vr.htm (August 26, 2010).

50 Richard Panek, "Out There," *New York Times Magazine*, March 11, 2007, http://www.nytimes.com/2007/03/11/magazine/11dark.t.html (August 26, 2010).

53 Kane, "The Dark Side."

57 Frank Borman, "Eyes Turned Skyward," Spacequotations.com, 2008–2010, http://spacequotations.com/earth.html (August 26, 2010).

60 Seema Singh, "We Want to See the First Objects That Were Formed after Big Bang: John C. Mather," *Wall Street Journal*, July 5, 2010, http://www.livemint.com/2010/07/04224808/We-want-to-see-the-first-objec.html (August 26, 2010).

64 Kristen Mack, "Columbia's Last Mission," *Houston Chronicle*, February 2, 2003, http://www.chron.com/CDA/archives/archive.mpl?id=2003_3623228 (August 26, 2010).

71 Space.com, "Rare Earth Debate Part 2: Alien Proximity," space.com, July 17, 2002, http://www.space.com/scienceastronomy/rare_earth_2_020717.html (August 26, 2010).

SELECTED BIBLIOGRAPHY

Ferris, Timothy. *Coming of Age in the Milky Way*. New York: HarperCollins Publishers, 2003.

Lawrence Livermore National Laboratory. FusEdWeb: Fusion Energy Education. 2010. http://fusedweb.llnl.gov/CPEP/Chart_Pages/5.Plasma4StateMatter.html (June 2010).

NASA. Joint Dark Energy Mission. 2010. http://jdem.gsfc.nasa.gov (June 2010).

——. NASA's Universe 101. 2010. http://map.gsfc.nasa.gov/universe (June 2010).

——. Planet Quest Mission: Kepler. 2010. http://planetquest.jpl.nasa.gov/missions/keplerMission.cfm (June 2010).

——. SIM Lite Mission. 2010. http://planetquest.jpl.nasa.gov/SIM/index.cfm (June 2010).

National Eath Science Teachers Association. Windows to the Universe. 2010. http://www.windows2universe.org (June 2010).

Pope, Damian. *The Mystery of Dark Matter*. Waterloo, ON: Perimeter Institute for Theoretical Physics, 2008.

SAO. Chandra Field Guide: Dark Matter. 2010. http://xrtpub.harvard.edu/xray_astro/dark_matter/index.html (June 2010).

SETI Institute. 2010. http://www.seti.org/Page.aspx?pid=1366 (June 2010).

Terrestrial Planet Finder Mission. 2010. http://www.terrestrial-planet-finder.com (June 2010).

Tyson, Neil deGrasse. *Death by Black Hole and Other Cosmic Quandaries*. New York: W. W. Norton and Company, 2007.

University of Maryland. MOND Pages. 2010. http://www.astro.umd.edu/~ssm/mond (June 2010).

Universe Today. 2010. http://www.universetoday.com (June 2010).

FURTHER READING AND WEBSITES

Books

Bortz, Fred. *Astrobiology*. Minneapolis: Lerner Publications Company, 2008. This title showcases the field of astrobiology—the study of how life developed on Earth and how it could exist on other planets.

Fleisher, Paul. *The Big Bang*. Minneapolis: Twenty-First Century Books, 2006. Explore the theory behind the big bang in this thorough introduction to the topic.

Hill, Steele, and Michael Carlowicz. *The Sun*. New York: Harry N. Abrams, 2006. This title includes amazing images of the Sun taken by space telescopes, along with descriptions of how the Sun works.

Jackson, Ellen, and Nic Bishop. *Mysterious Universe: Supernovae, Dark Energy, and Black Holes*. New York: Houghton Mifflin Books for Children, 2008. This book describes the day-to-day trials and triumphs of an astronomer as he searches for supernovae and evidence of dark energy.

McPherson, Stephanie Sammartino. *Ordinary Genius: The Story of Albert Einstein*. Minneapolis: Twenty-First Century Books, 1995. Einstein's theories of relativity have helped scientists better understand the mysteries of the universe. This book tells his story.

Miller, Ron. *Stars and Galaxies*. Minneapolis: Twenty-First Century Books, 2006. Miller offers a guide to many wonders of the universe. Photos and illustrations complement the text.

Nicolson, Iain. *Dark Side of the Universe: Dark Matter, Dark Energy, and the Fate of the Cosmos*. Johns Hopkins University Press, 2007. Through interesting descriptions and pictures, this book describes why scientists think most of our universe is dark.

Silverstein, Alvin, Virginia Silverstein, and Laura Silverstein Nunn. *The Universe*. Minneapolis: Twenty-First Century Books, 2009. Take an in-depth look at the worlds beyond our own, including planets and different kinds of stars.

Skurzynski, Gloria. *Are We Alone? Scientists Search for Life in Space*. Washington, DC: National Geographic Children's Books, 2004. This book describes the science and the scientists behind the search for extraterrestrial life.

Websites

Inside Black Holes

http://jila.colorado.edu/~ajsh/insidebh/index.html

This site contains computer visualizations of what a person would see as he or she passed into a black hole.

NASA Missions Homepage

http://www.nasa.gov/missions/index.html

Learn about upcoming NASA missions to study black holes, explore the mysteries of dark matter and dark energy, and find exoplanets.

NASA's Imagine the Universe!

http://imagine.gsfc.nasa.gov/index.html

This site provides answers to all your hard questions about the universe, written by NASA scientists.

The Particle Adventure

http://www.particleadventure.org

Everything you want to know about matter and subatomic particles is offered here.

SOHO: The Solar and Heliospheric Observatory

http://sohowww.nascom.nasa.gov/home.html

This site is a great resource for up-to-the-minute photographs of and information about the Sun.

Space.com

http://www.space.com

Here you'll find the latest news on everything related to space.

INDEX

ABOUT THE AUTHOR

D. J. Ward lives in Elizabeth, Colorado, with his wife and two sons. He teaches high school physics, geology, and astronomy. Ward is active in his local church and enjoys hiking with his family, bicycling, playing basketball, and playing bass guitar (but never all at the same time).